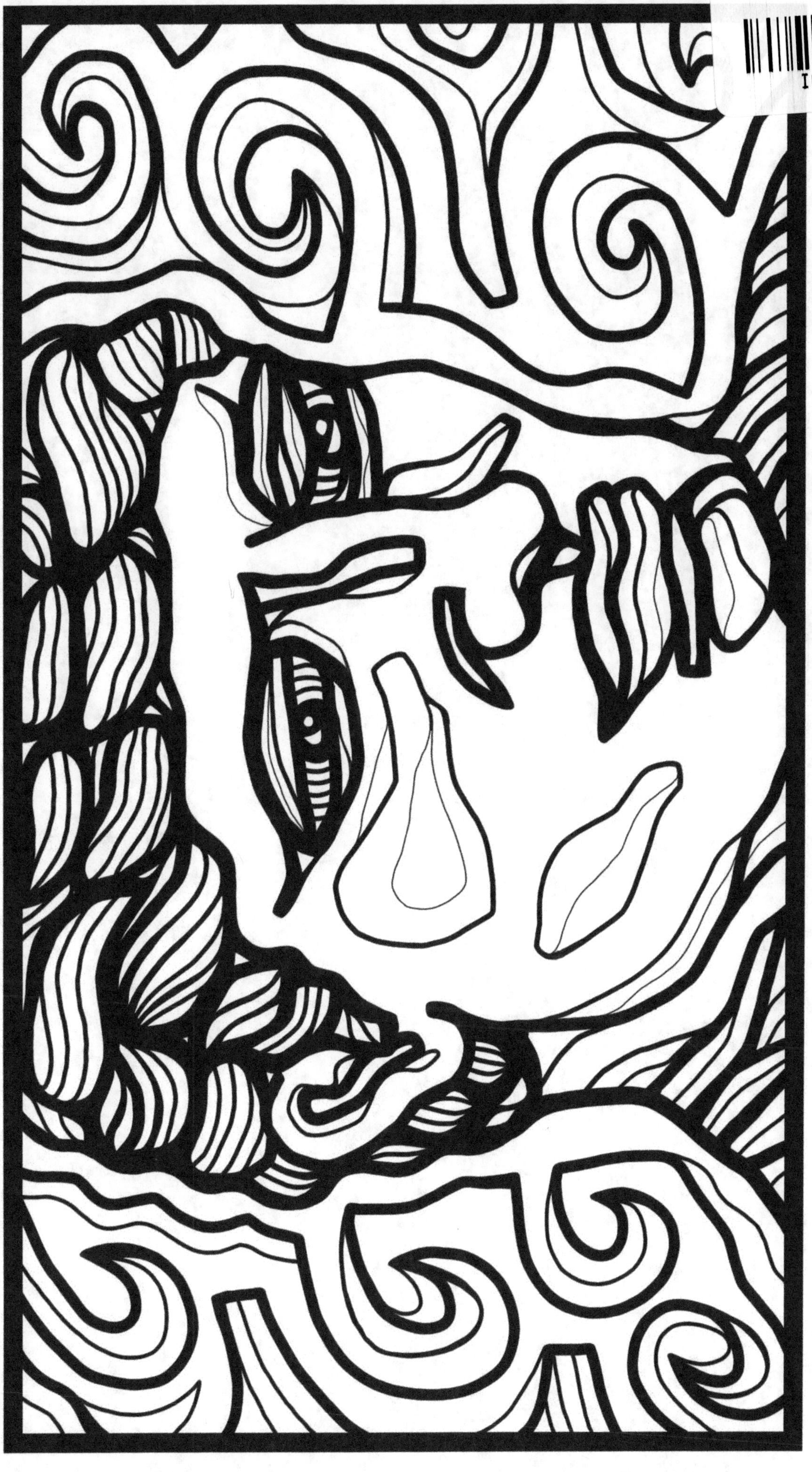

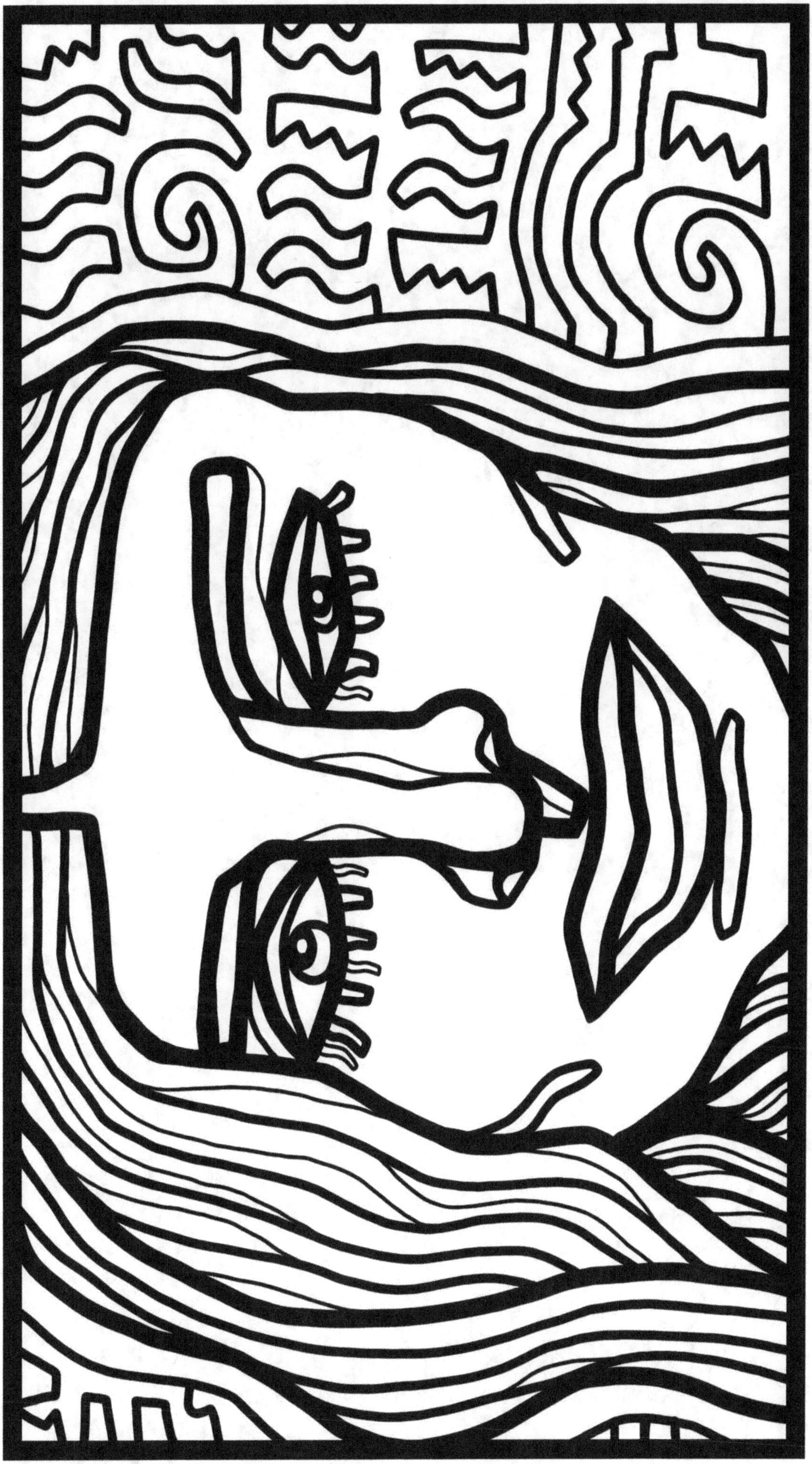

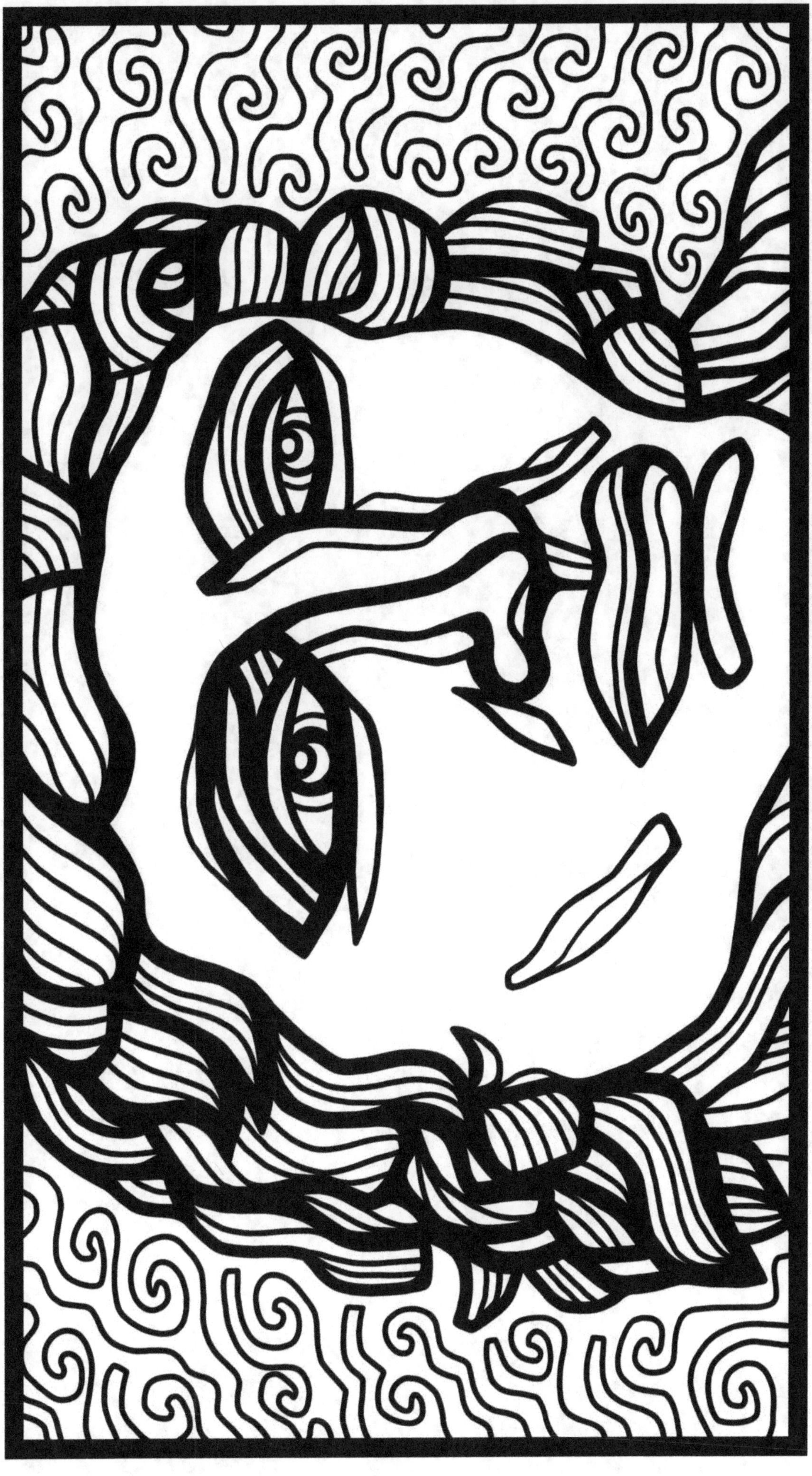

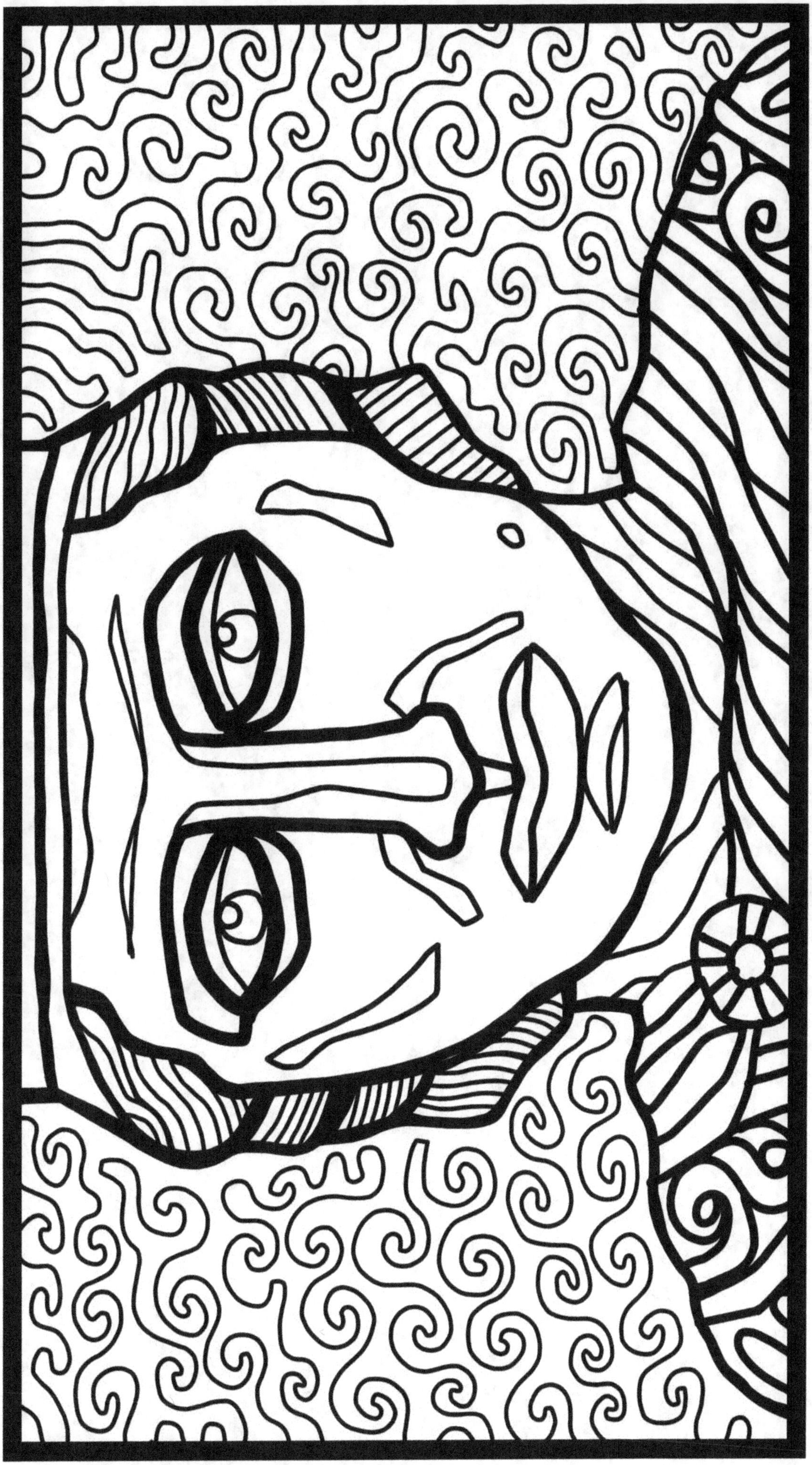

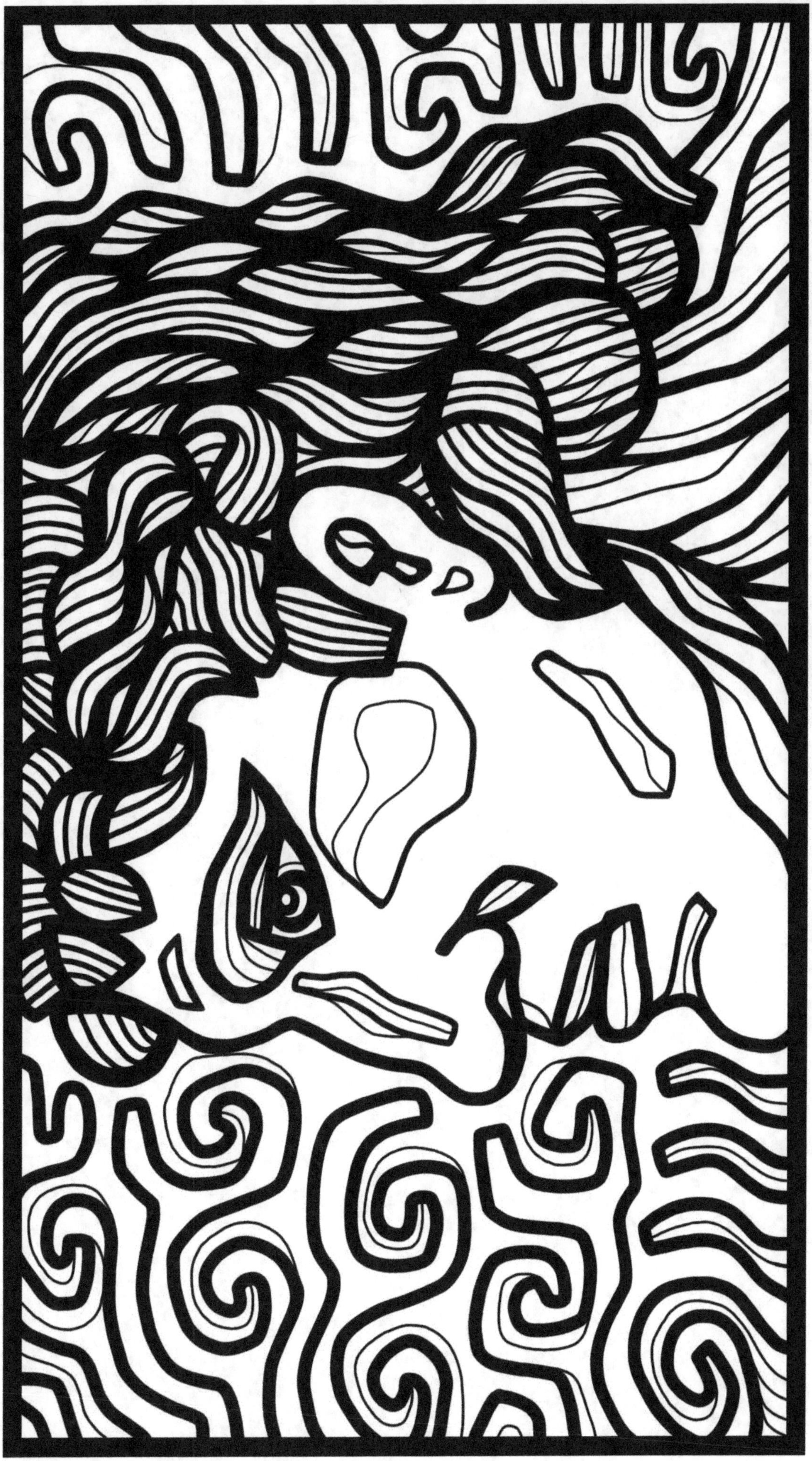

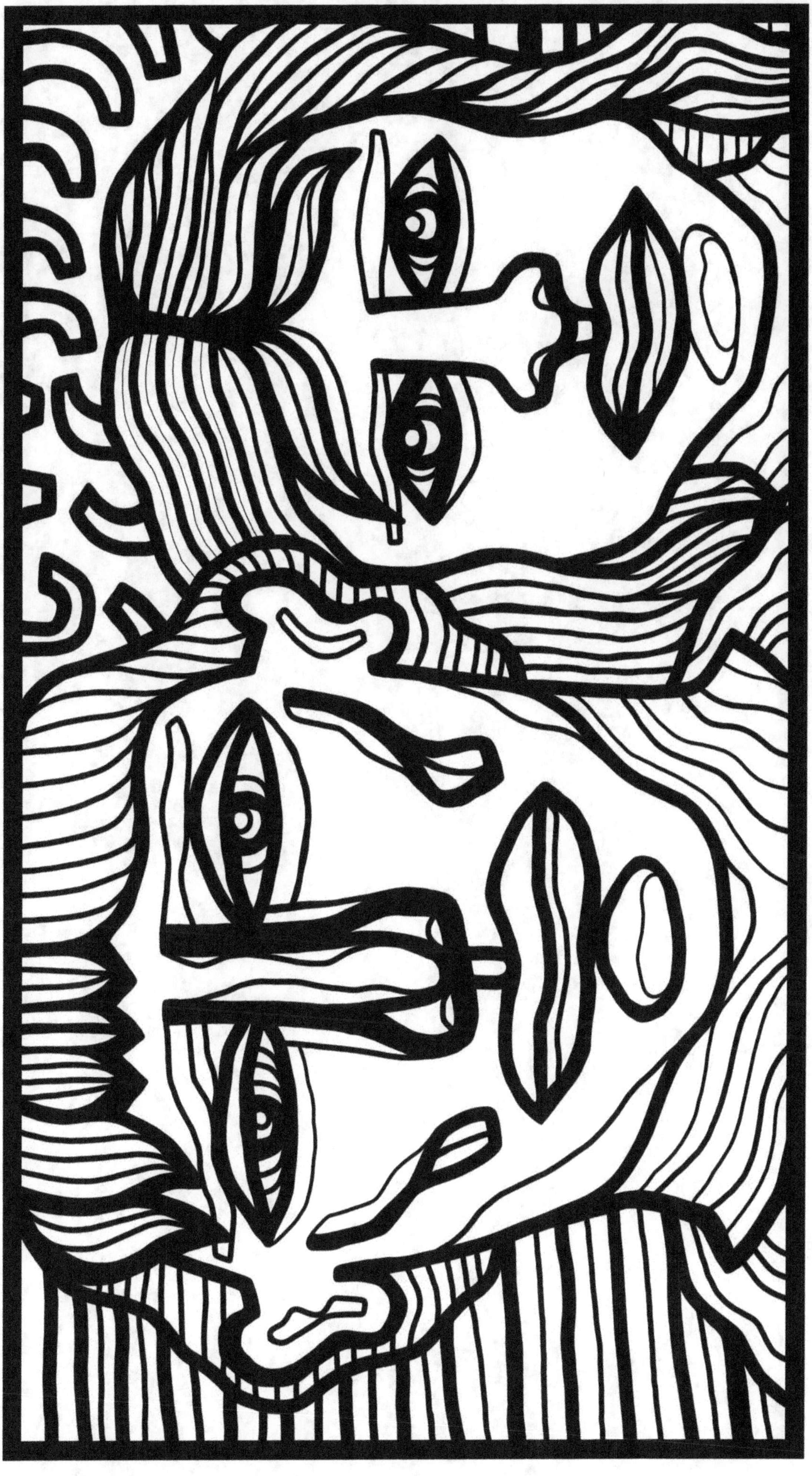

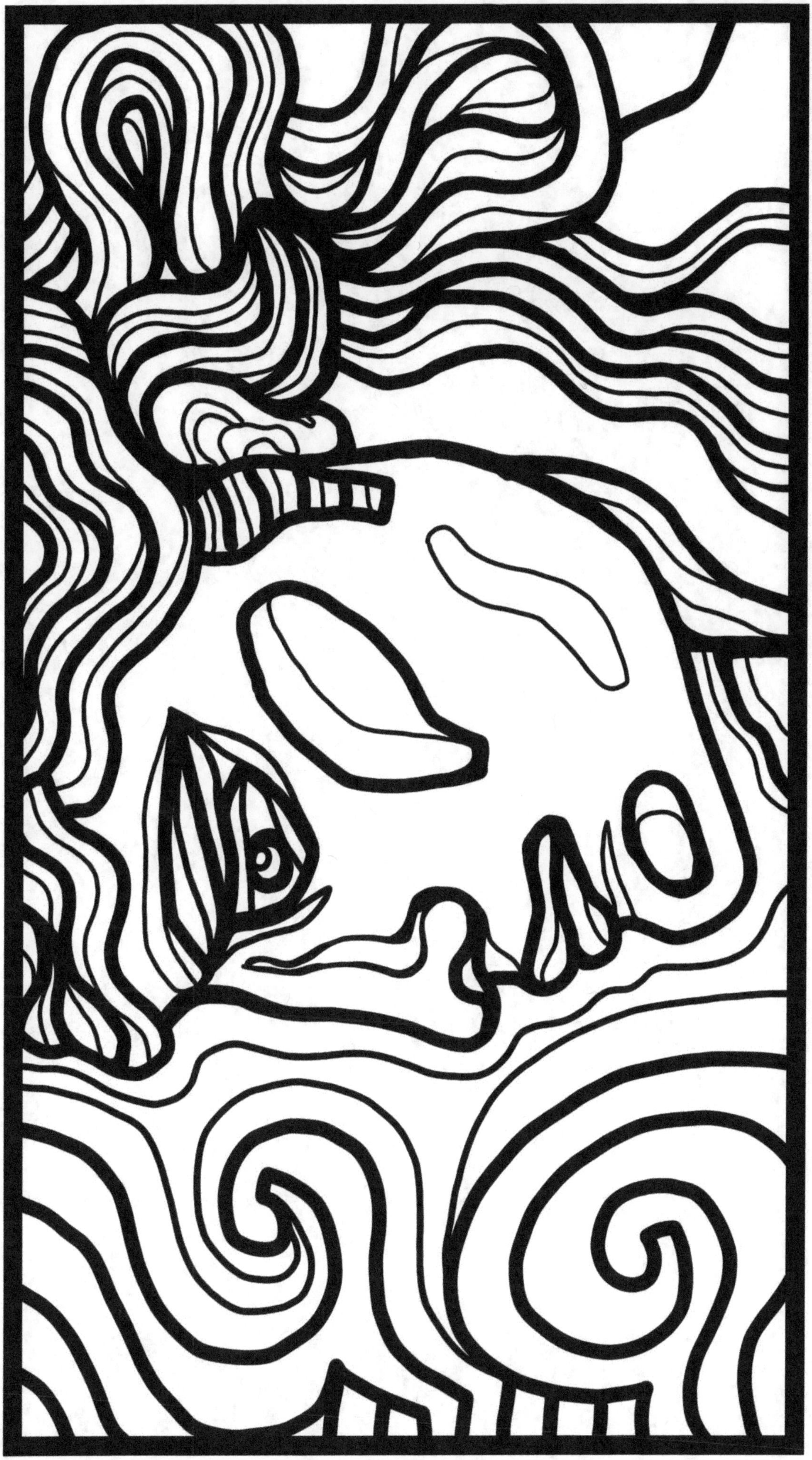

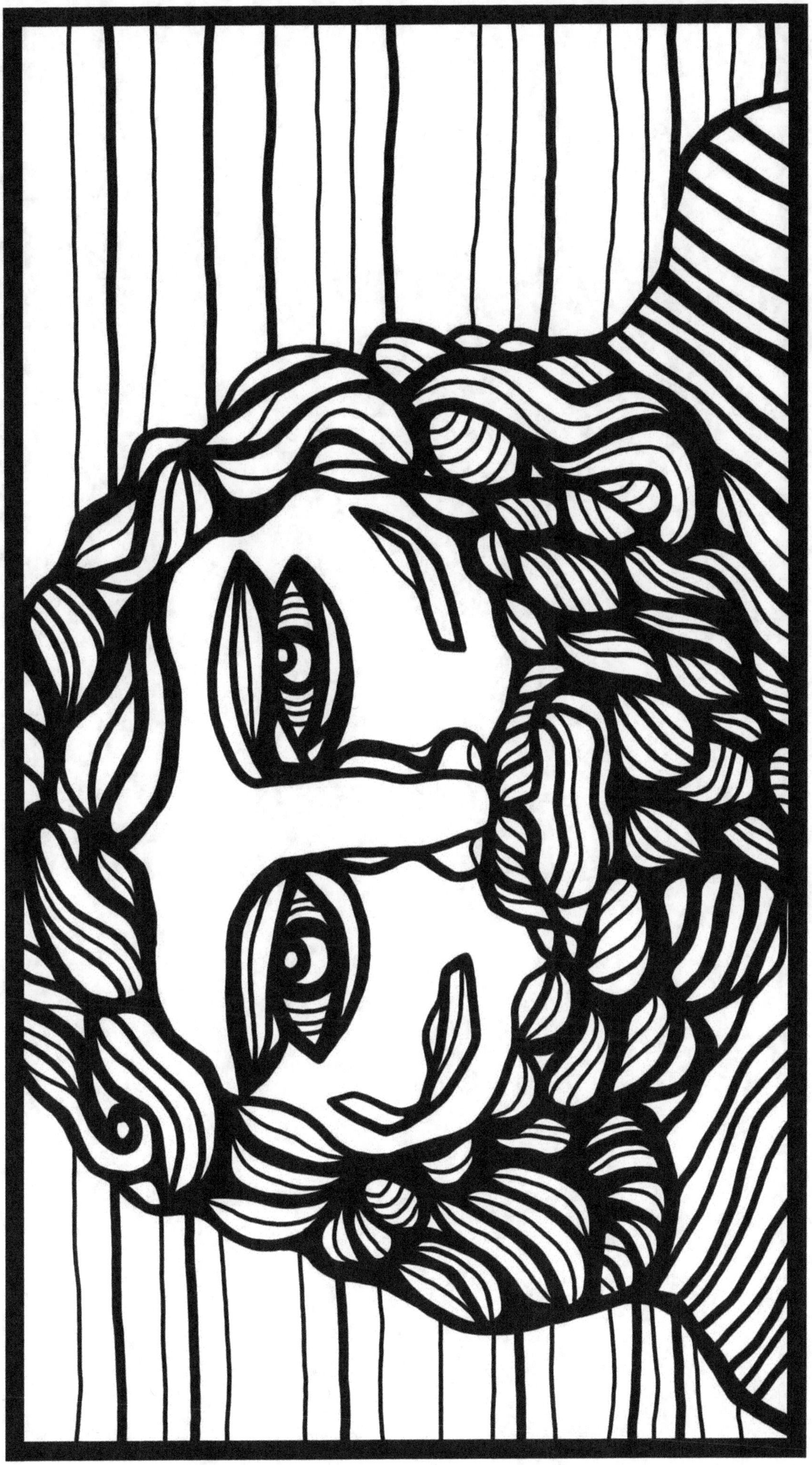

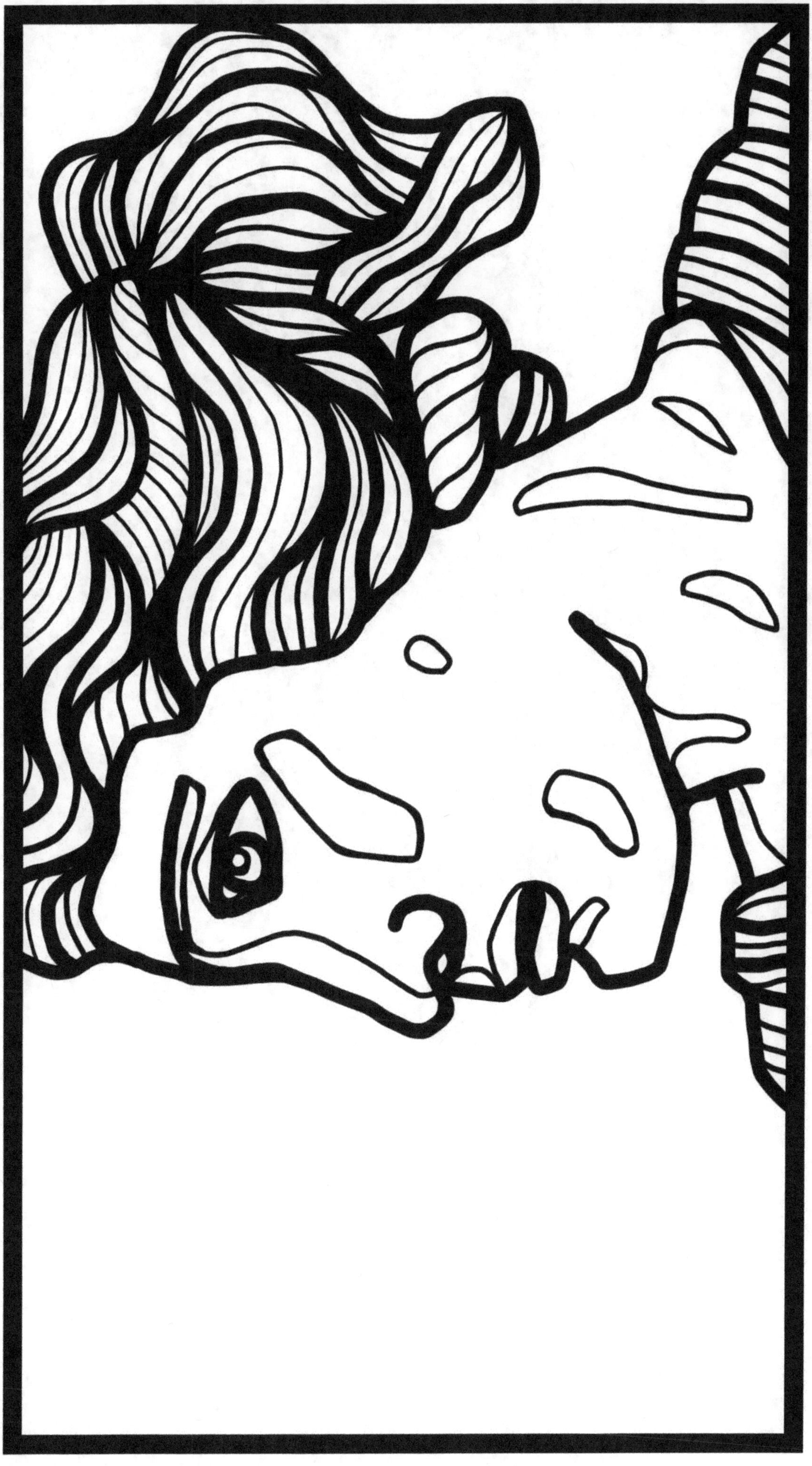

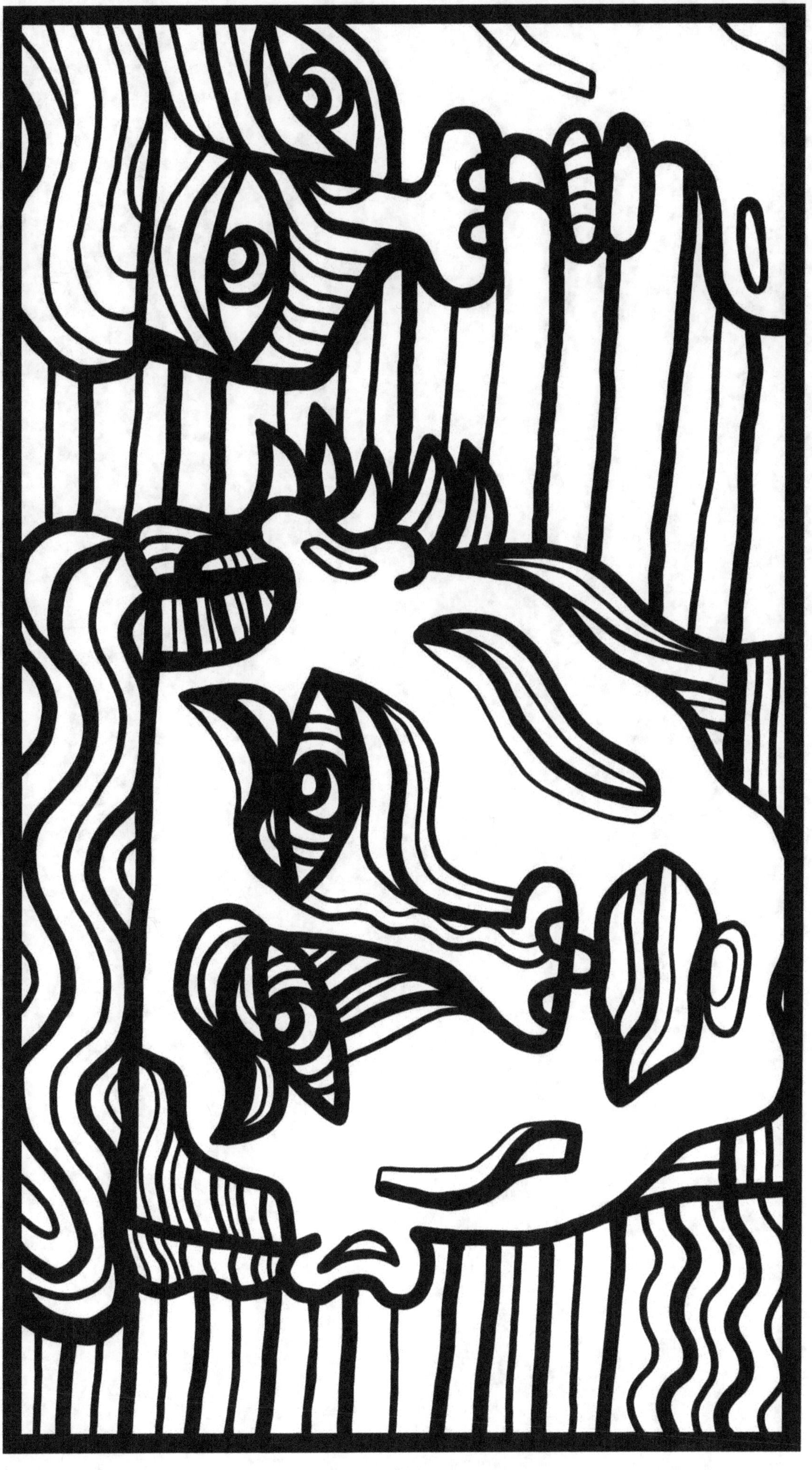

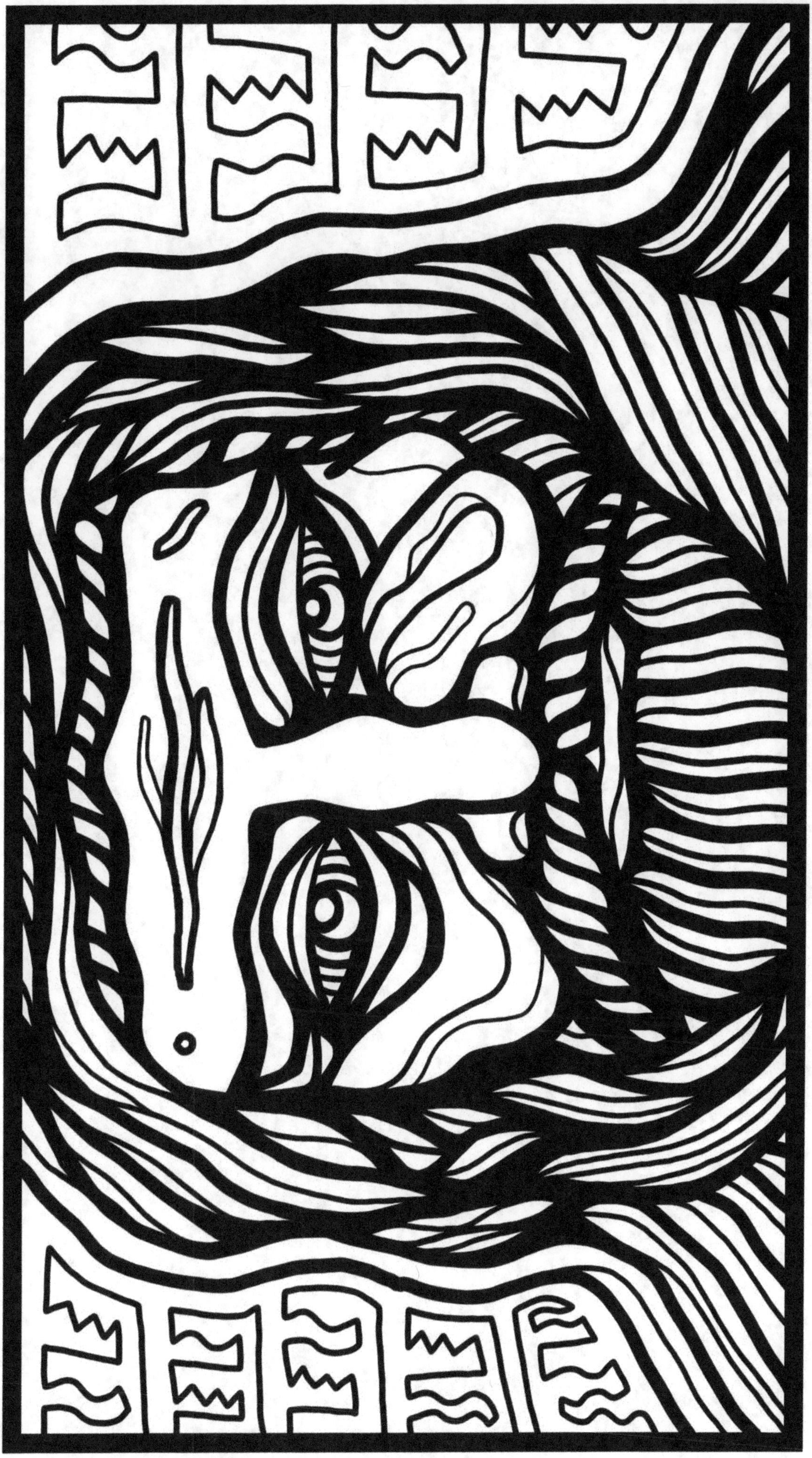

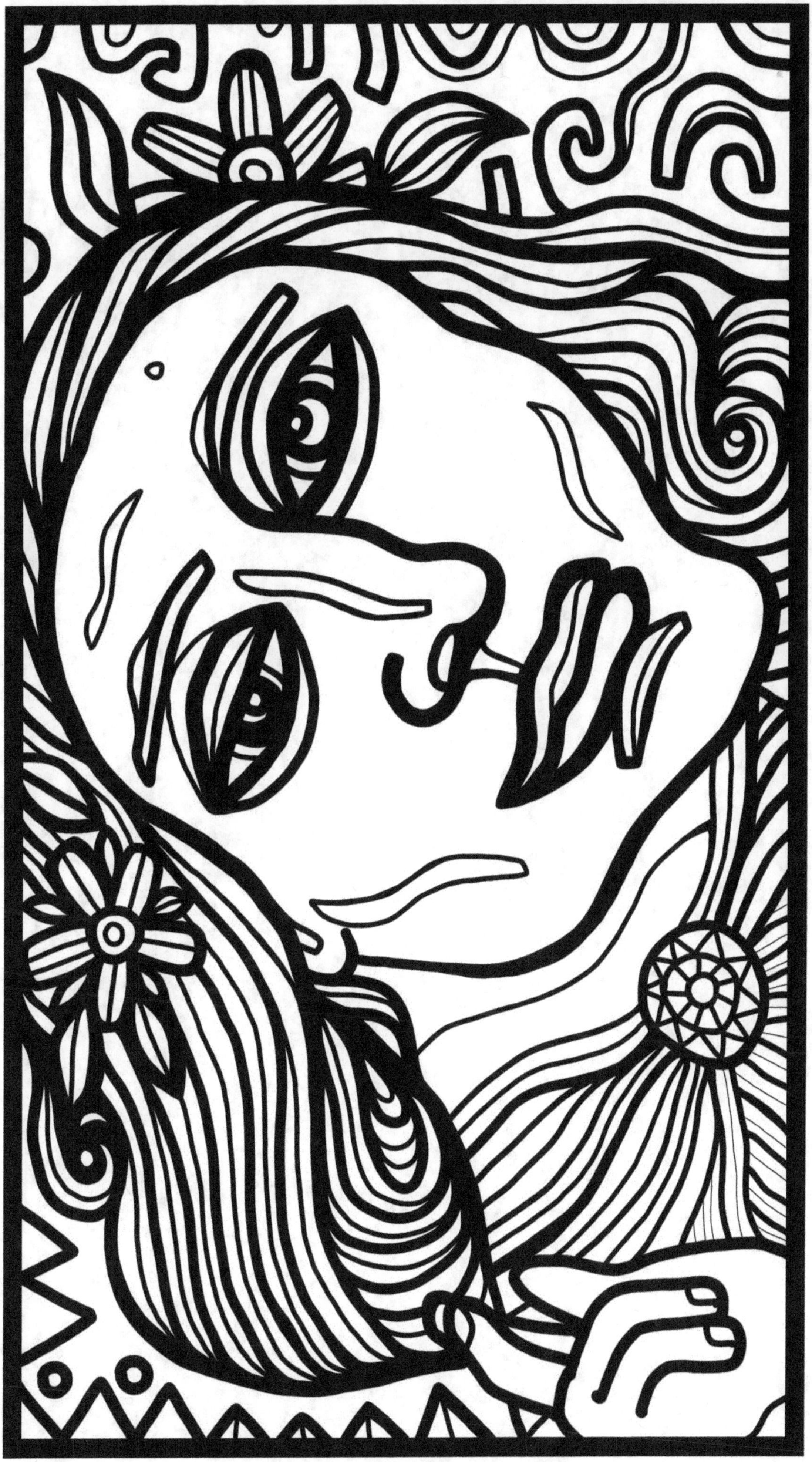

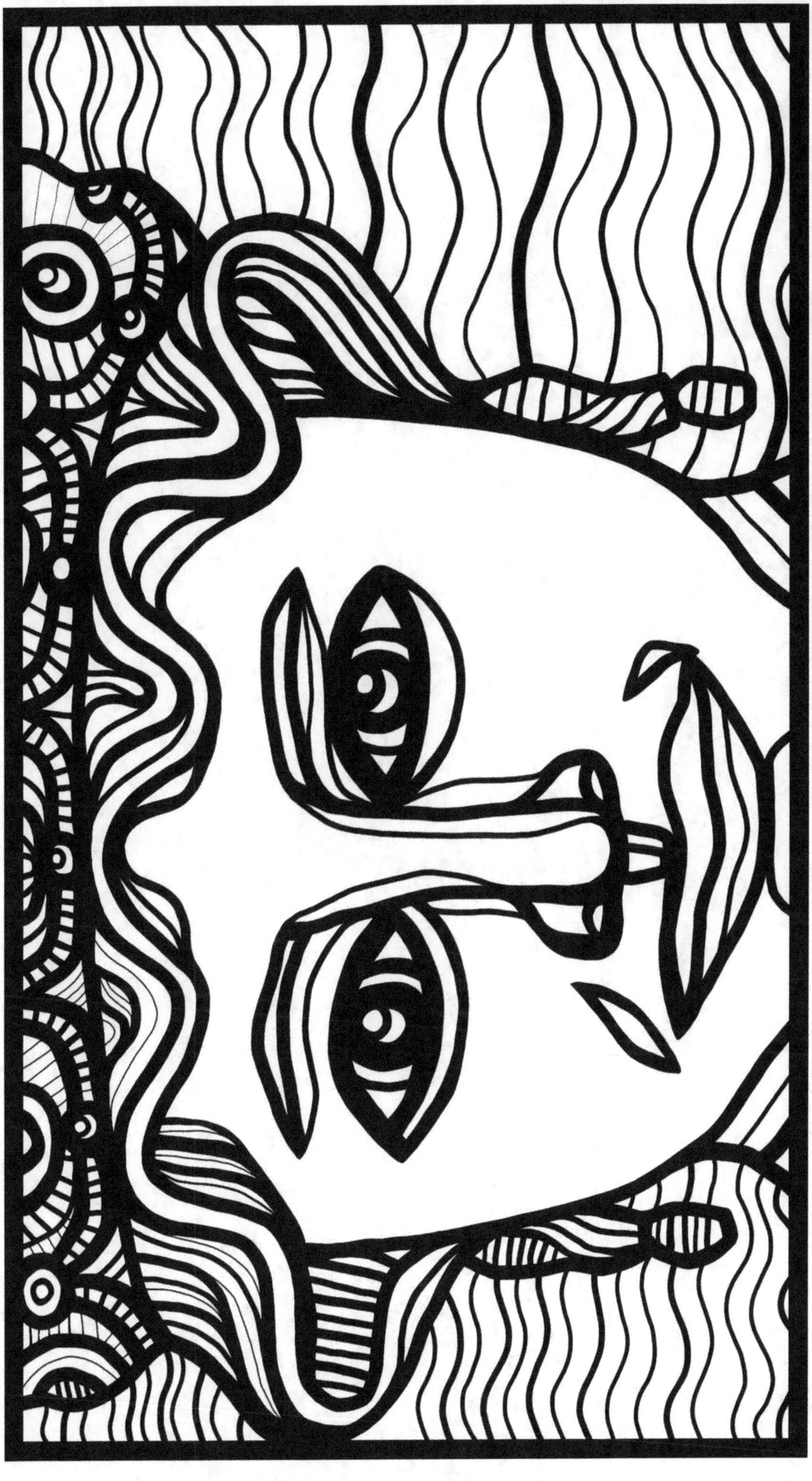

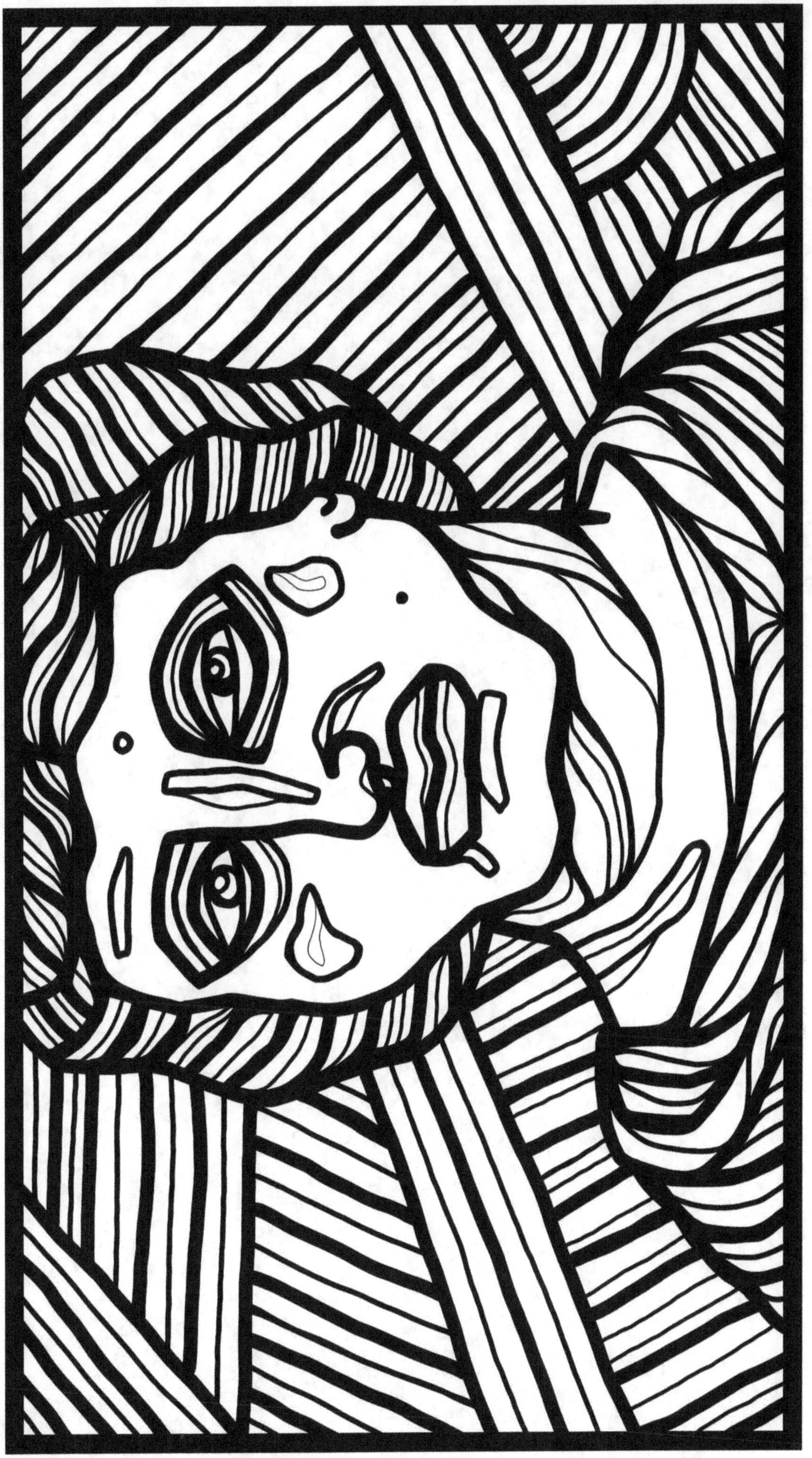

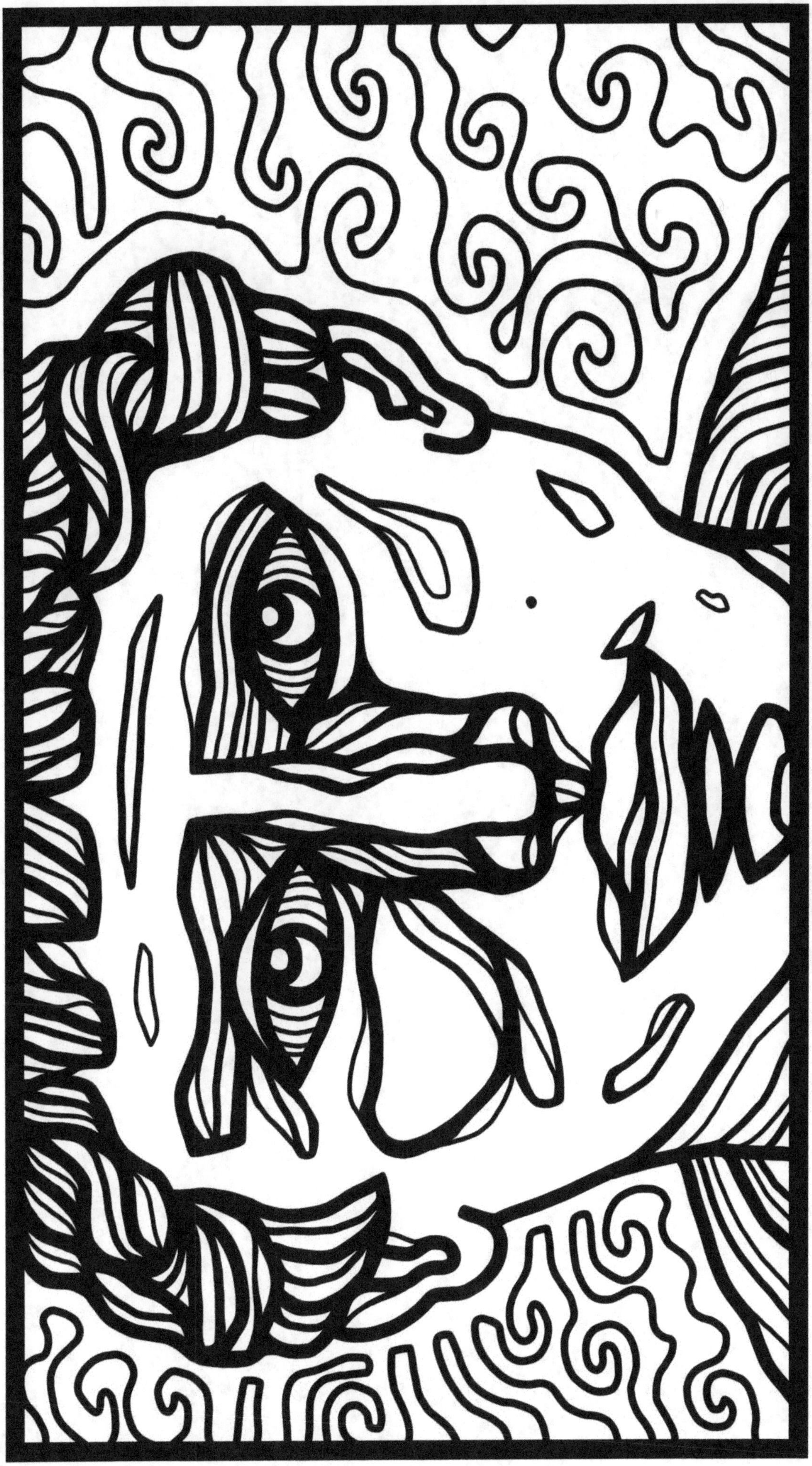

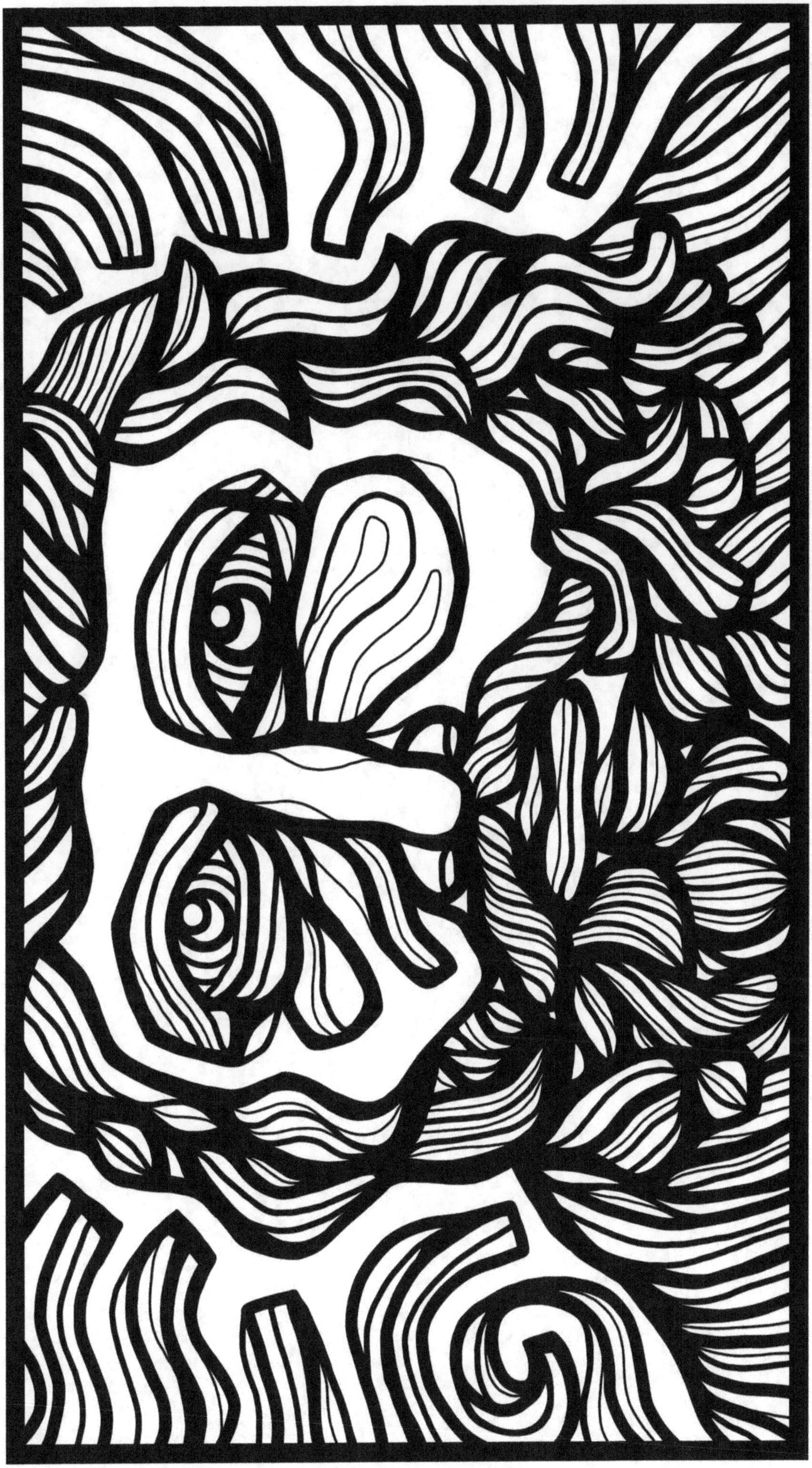

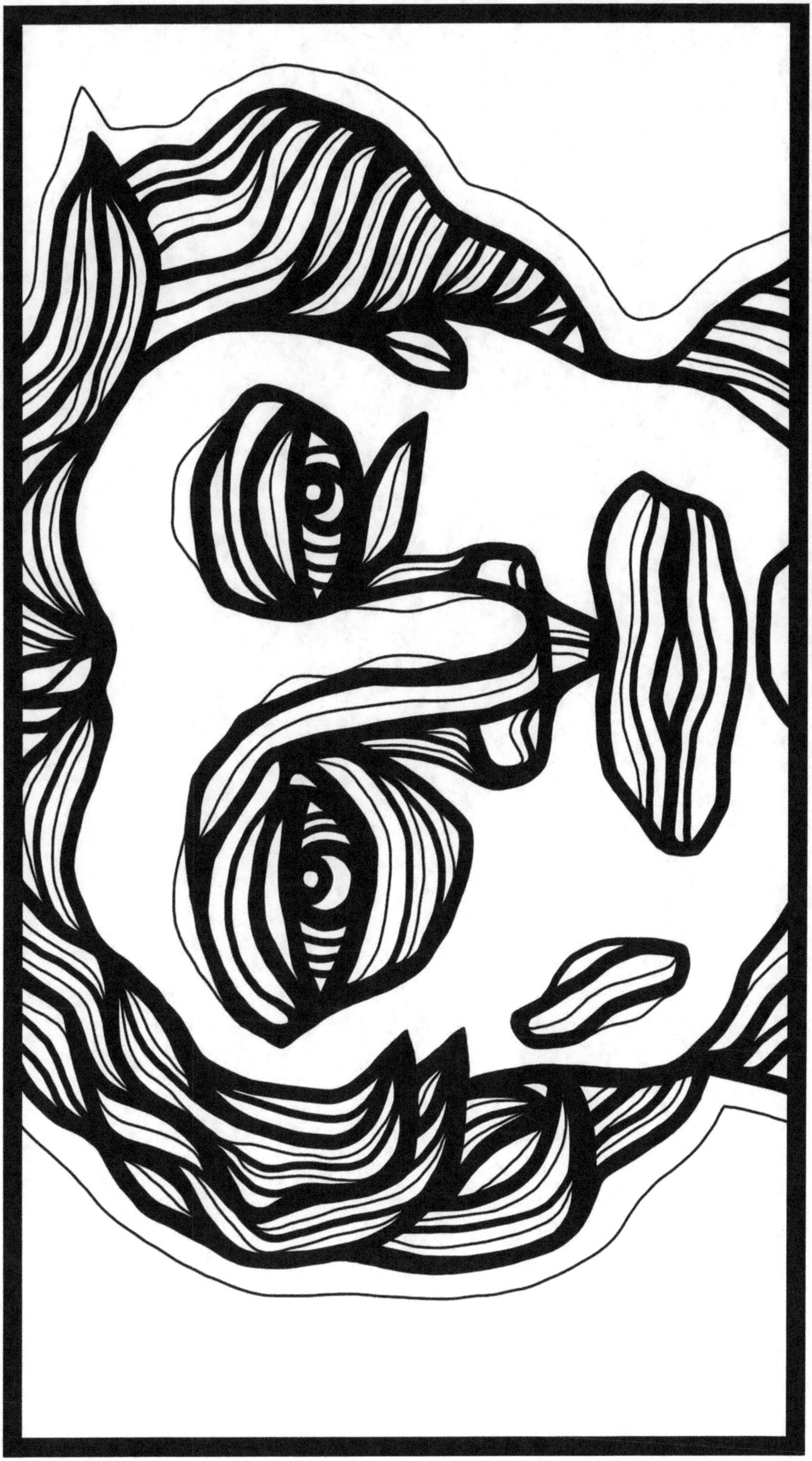

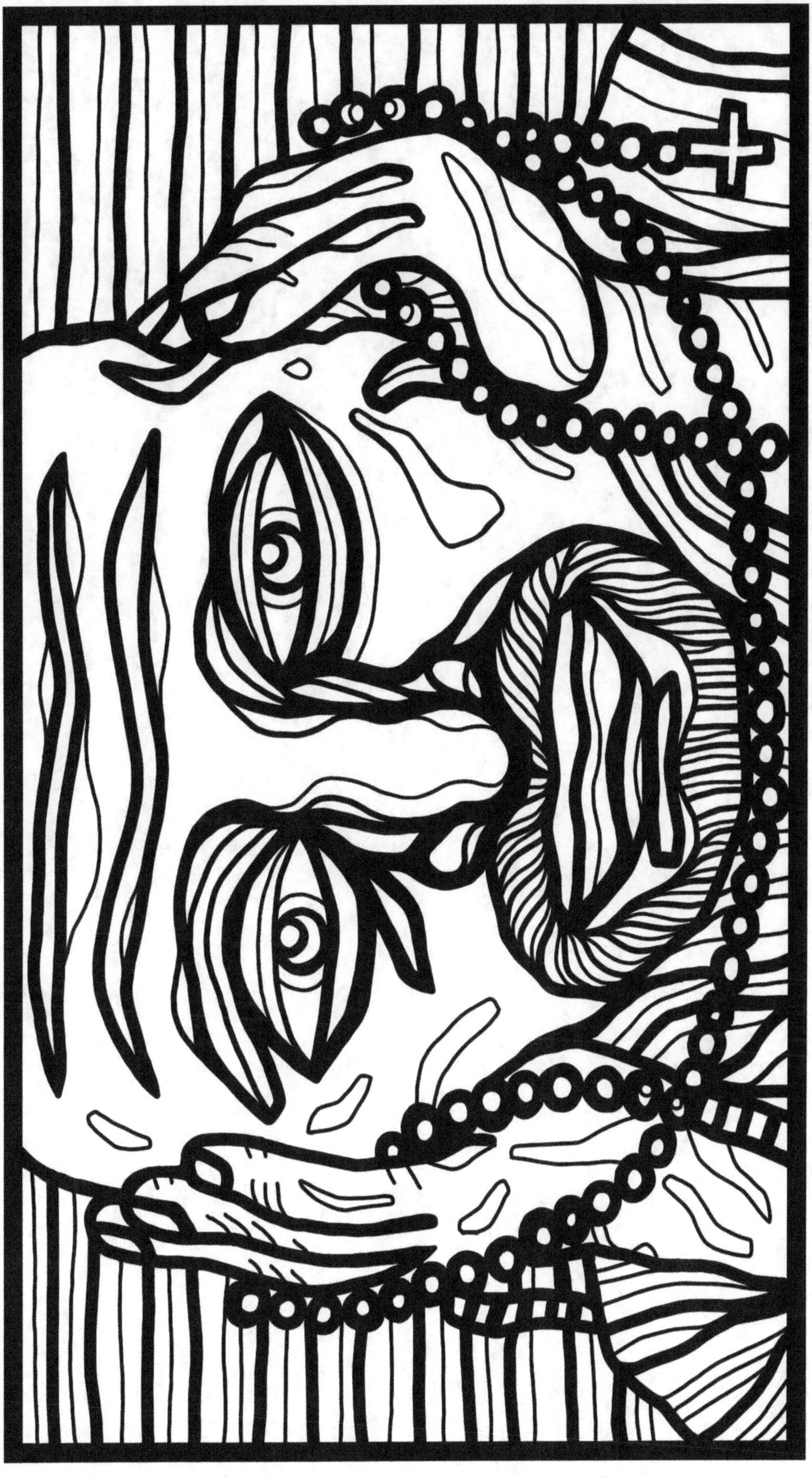

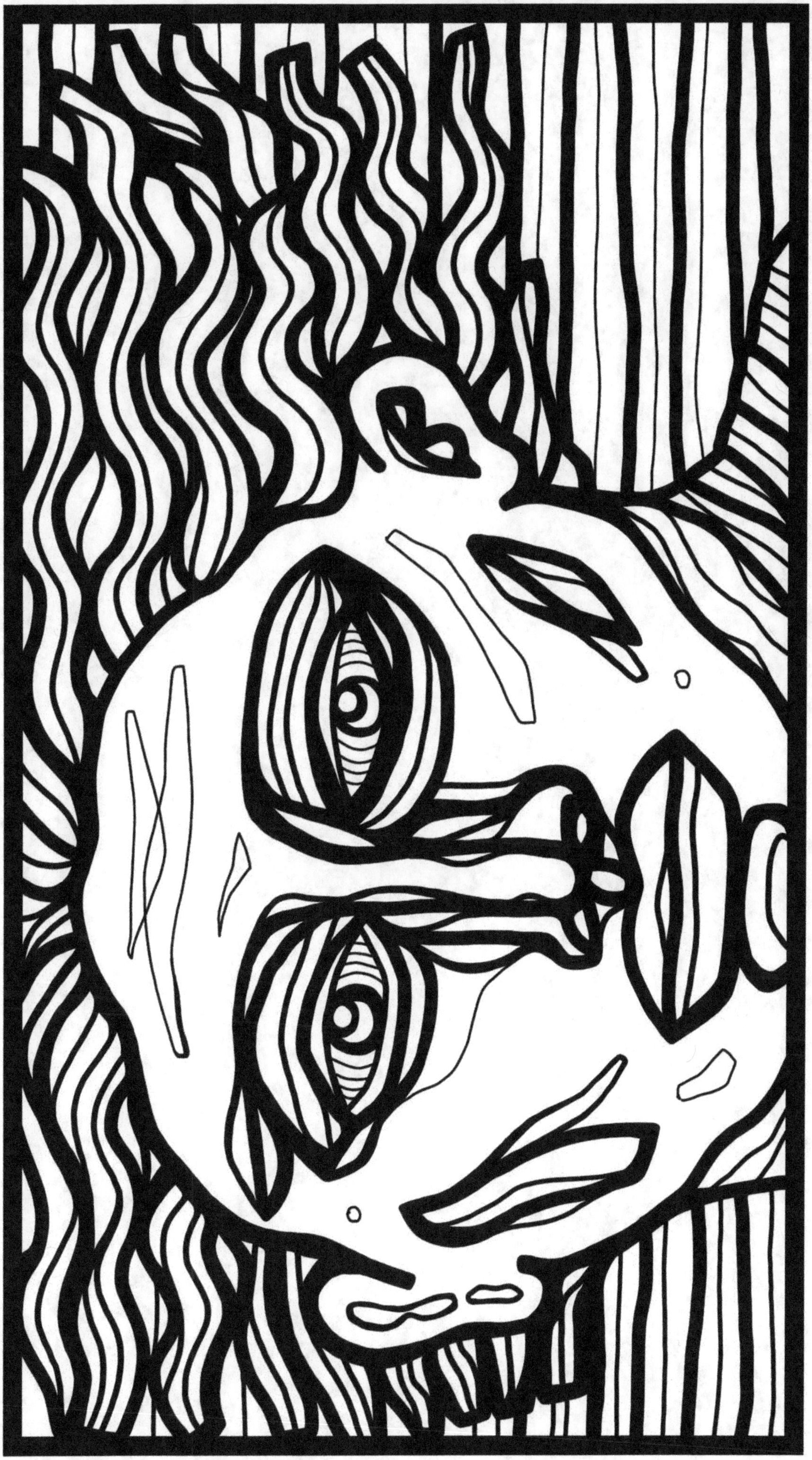

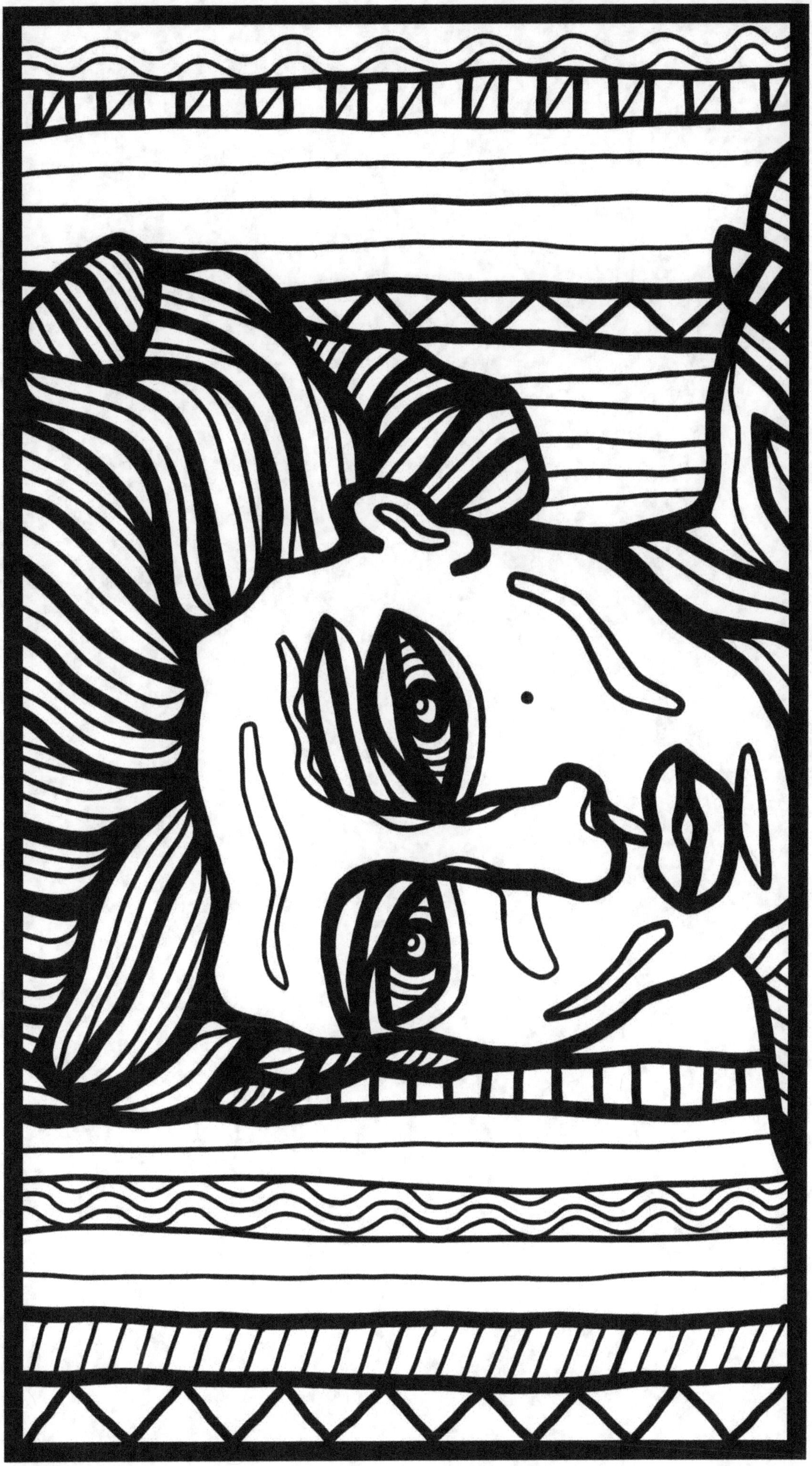

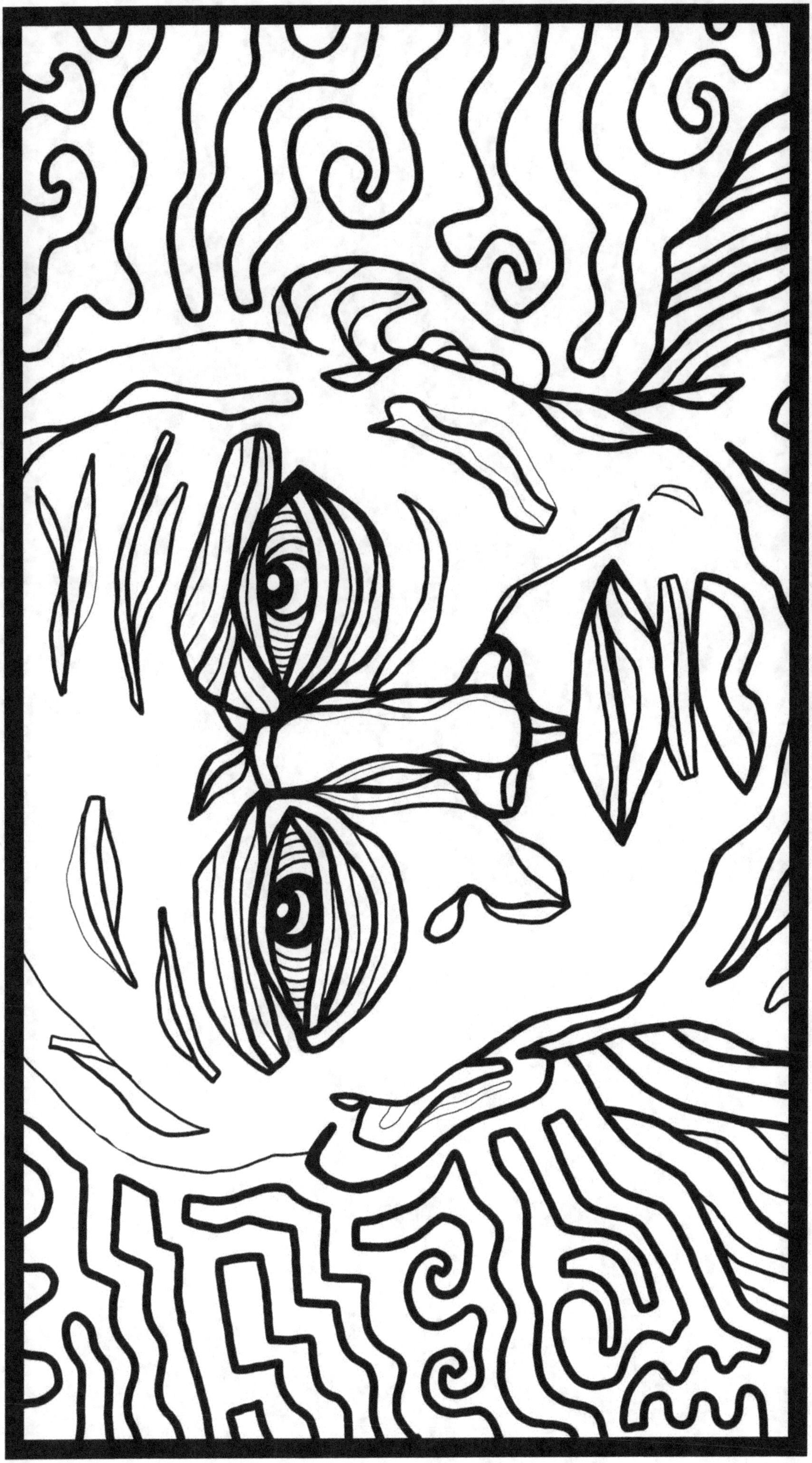

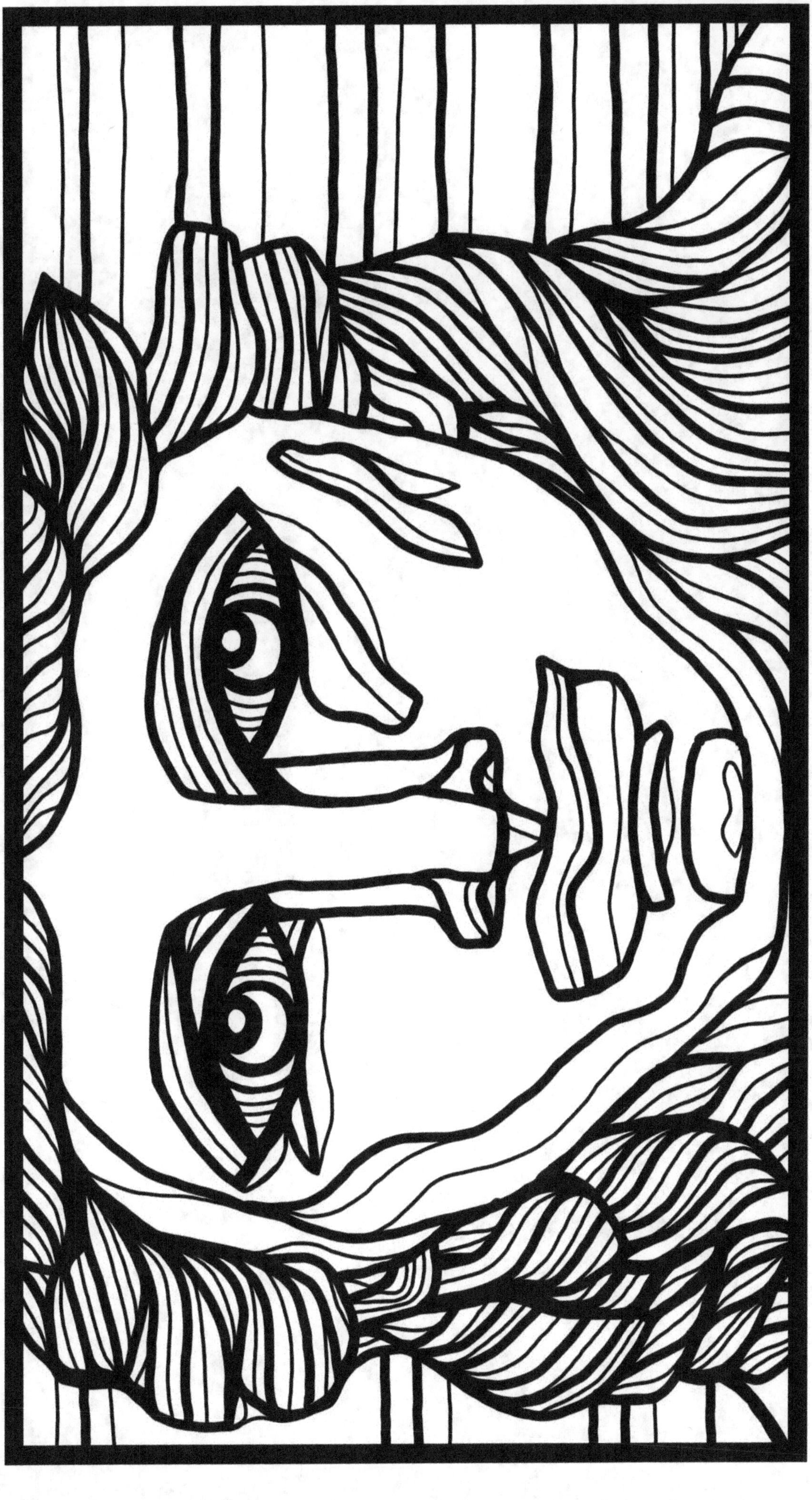

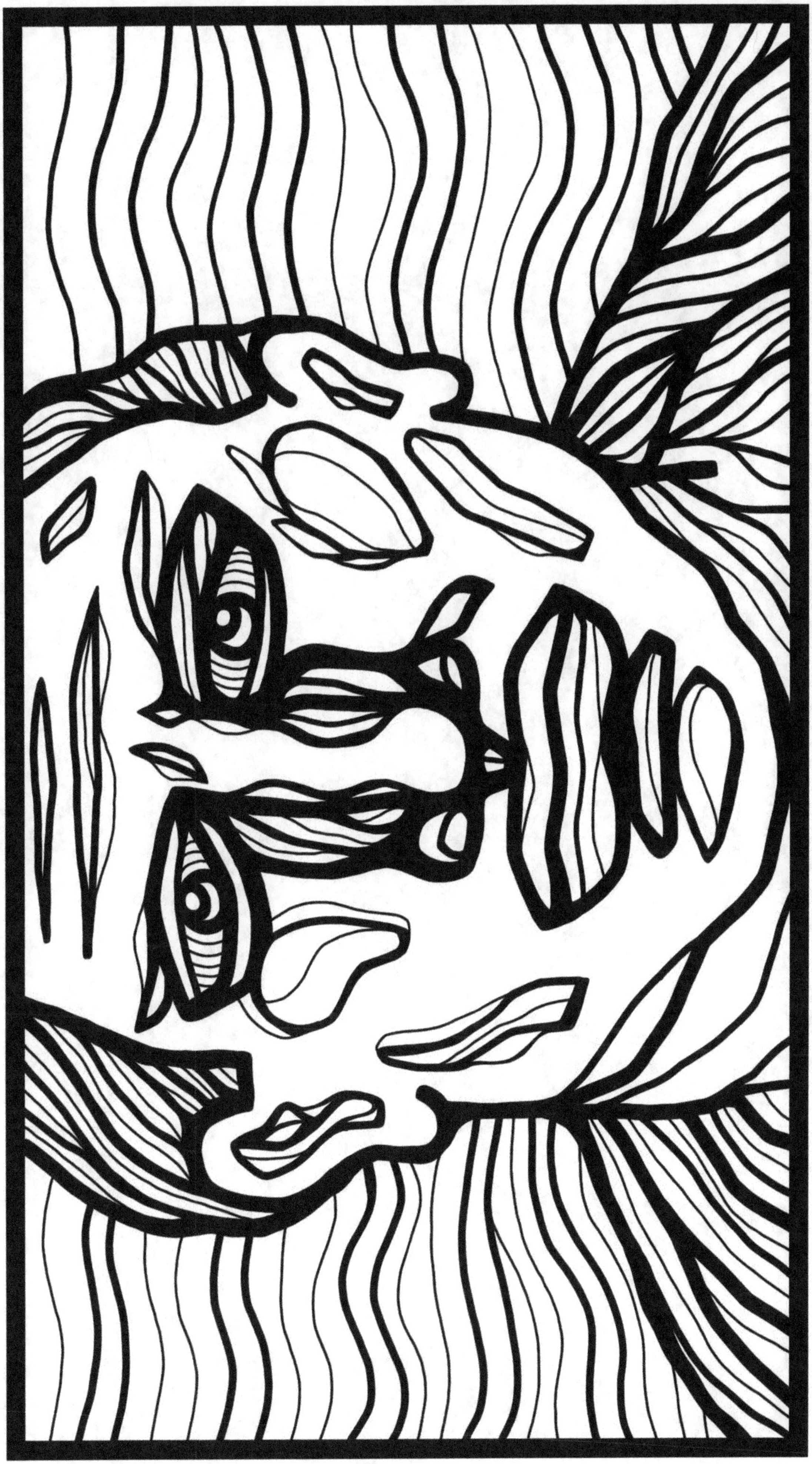

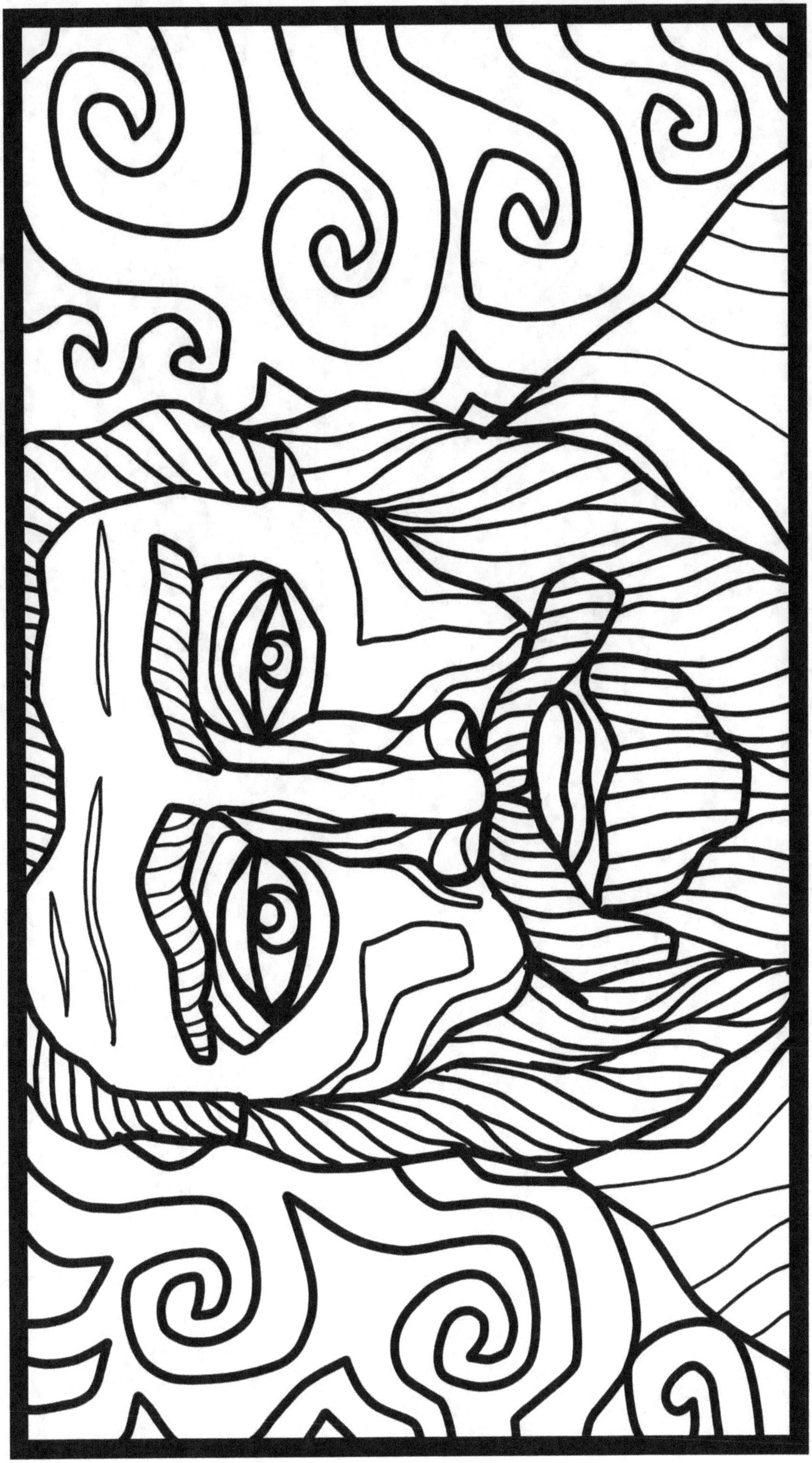

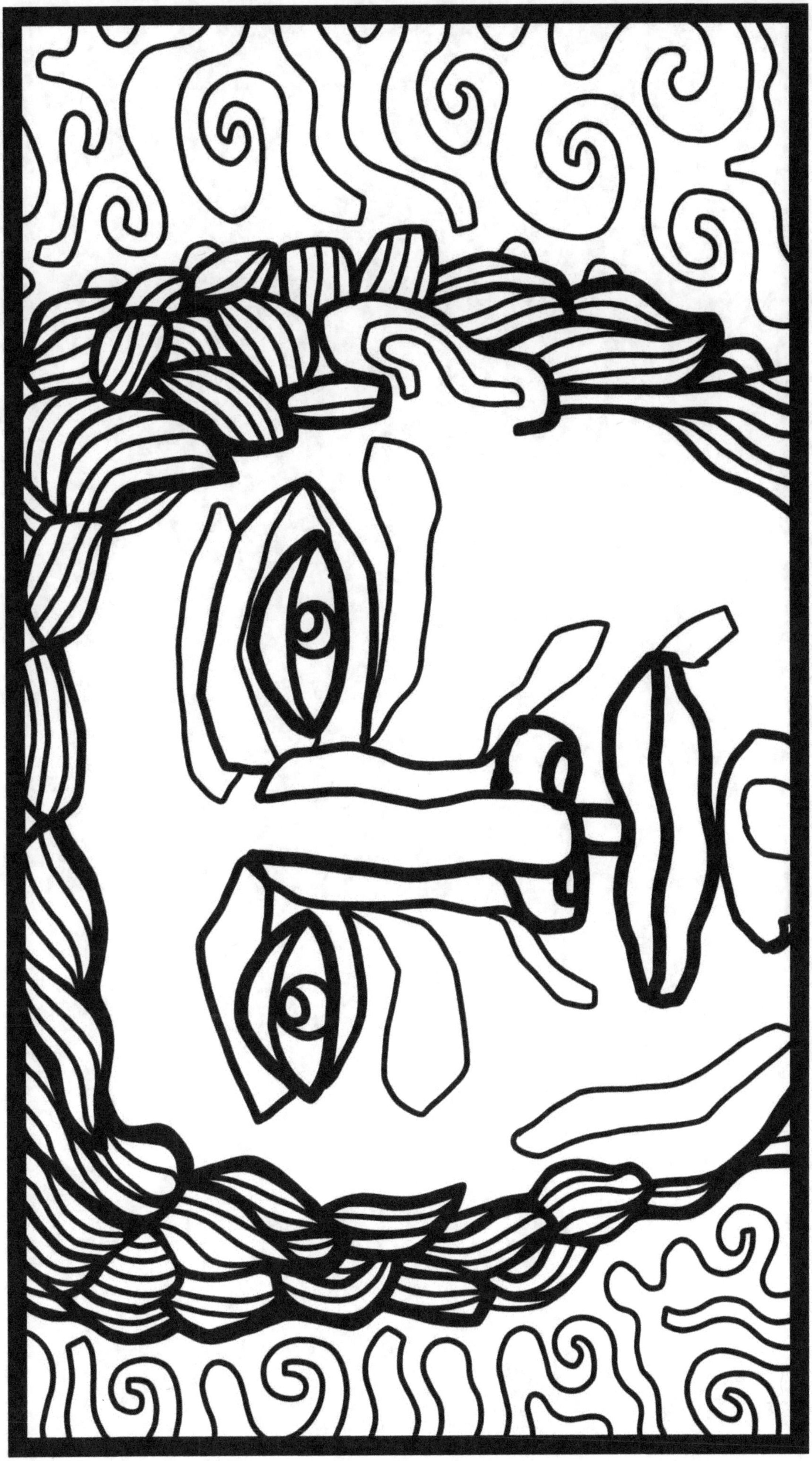

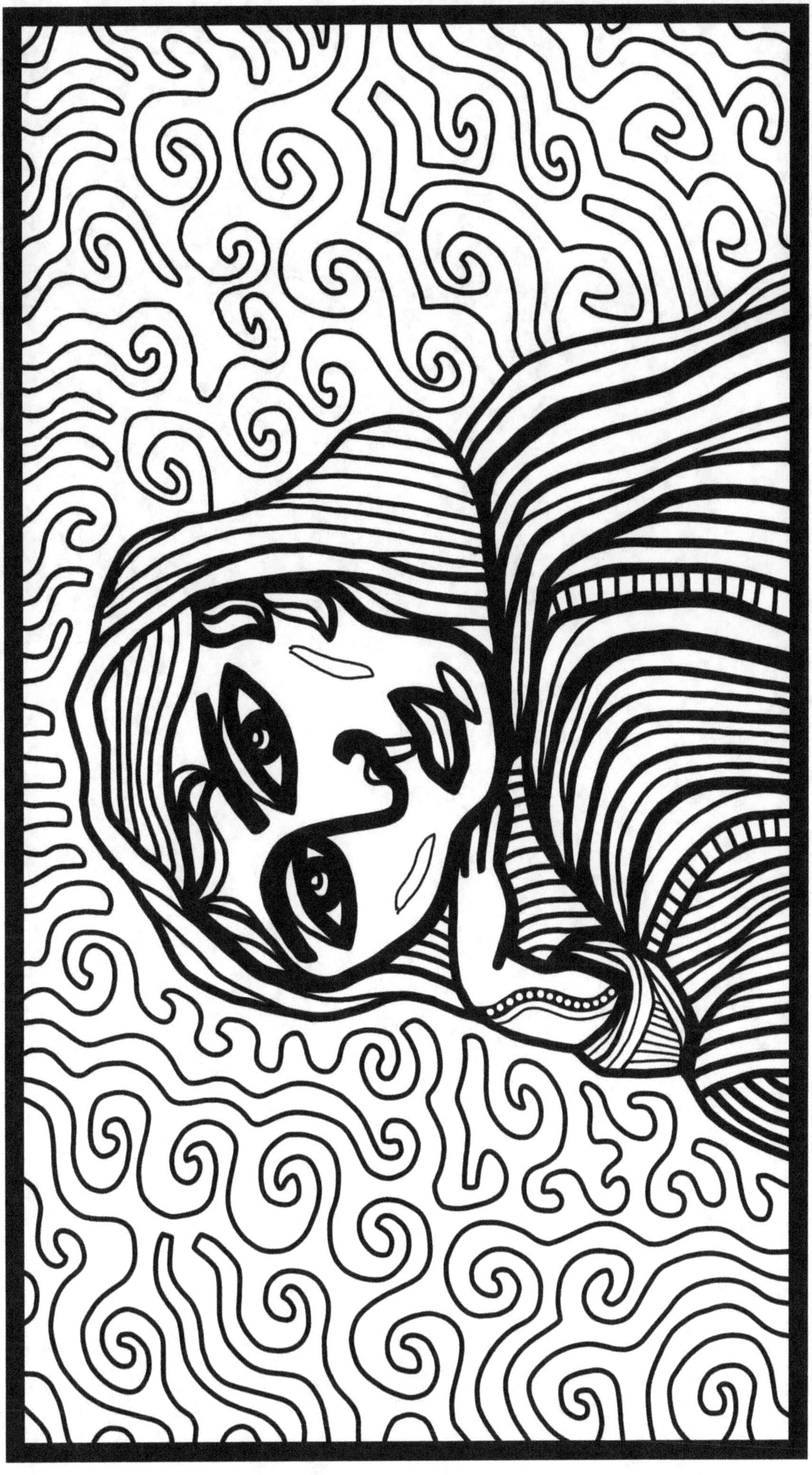

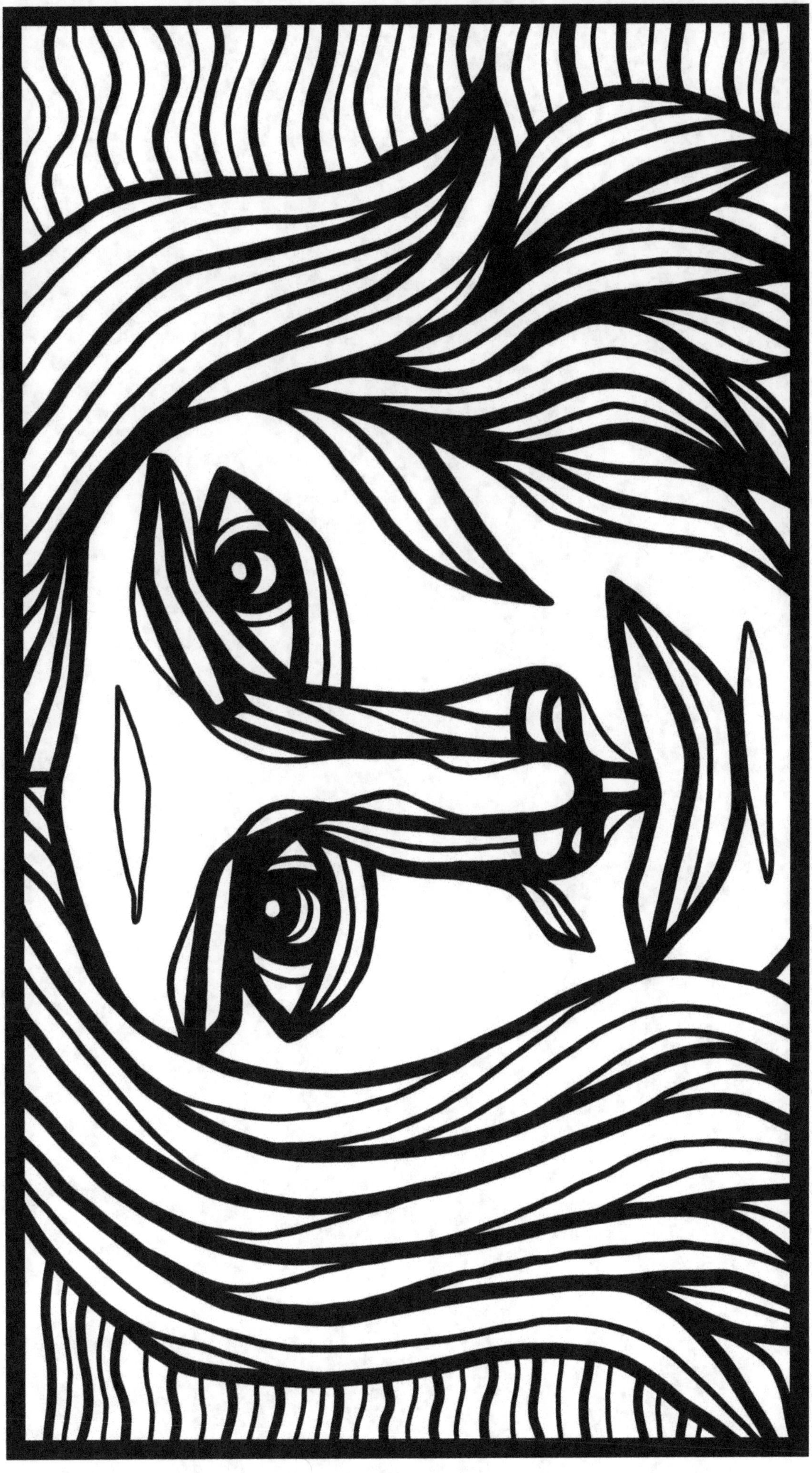

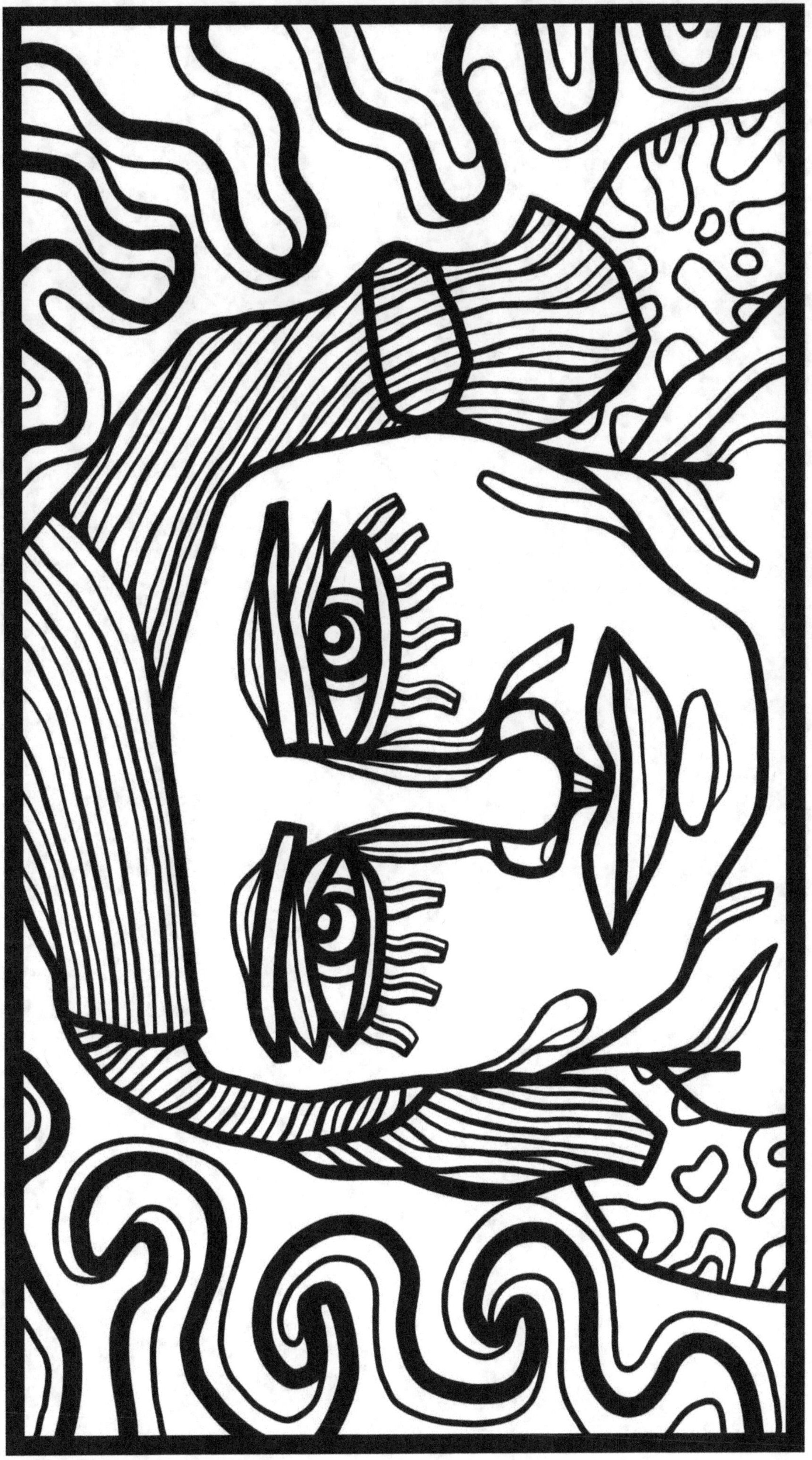

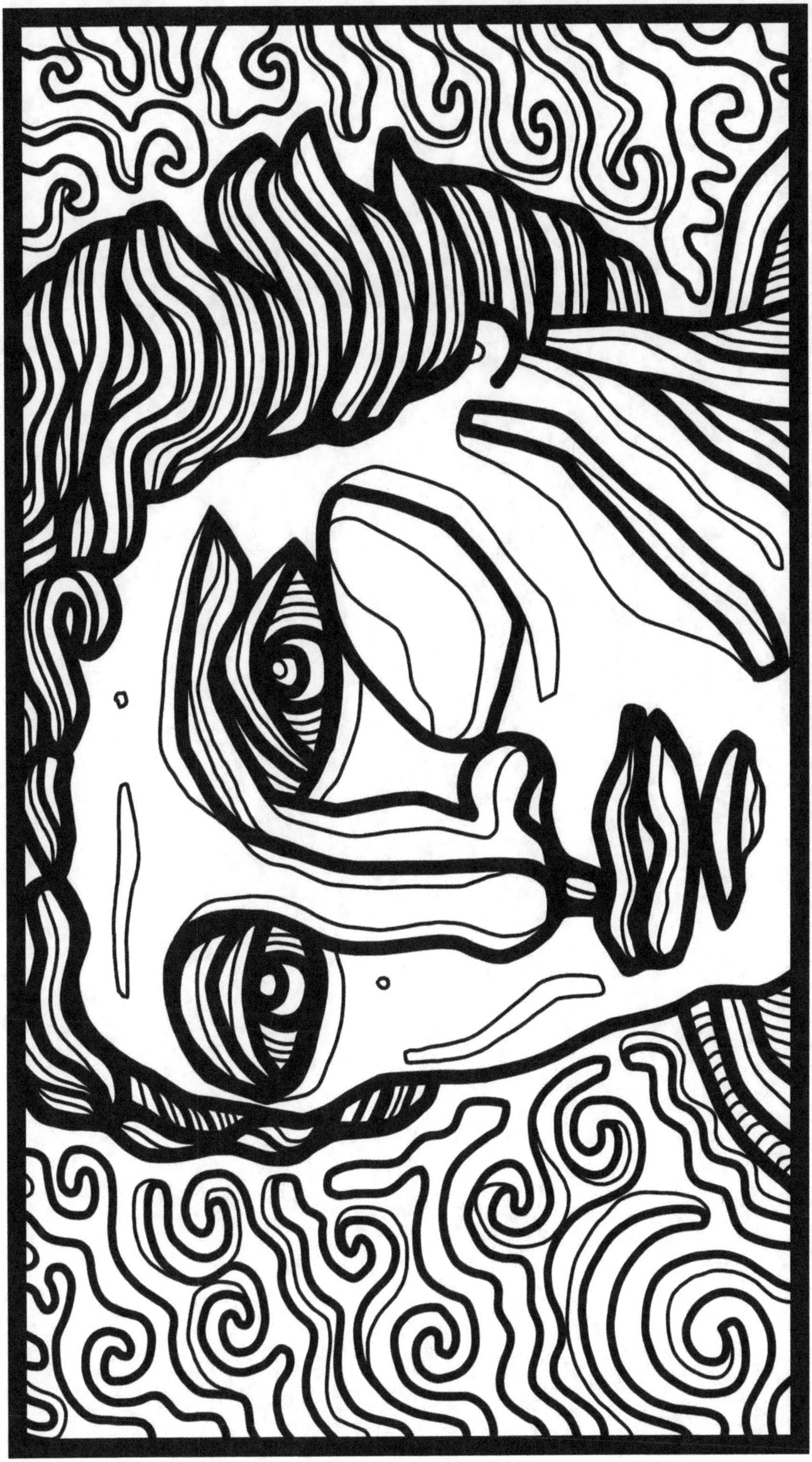

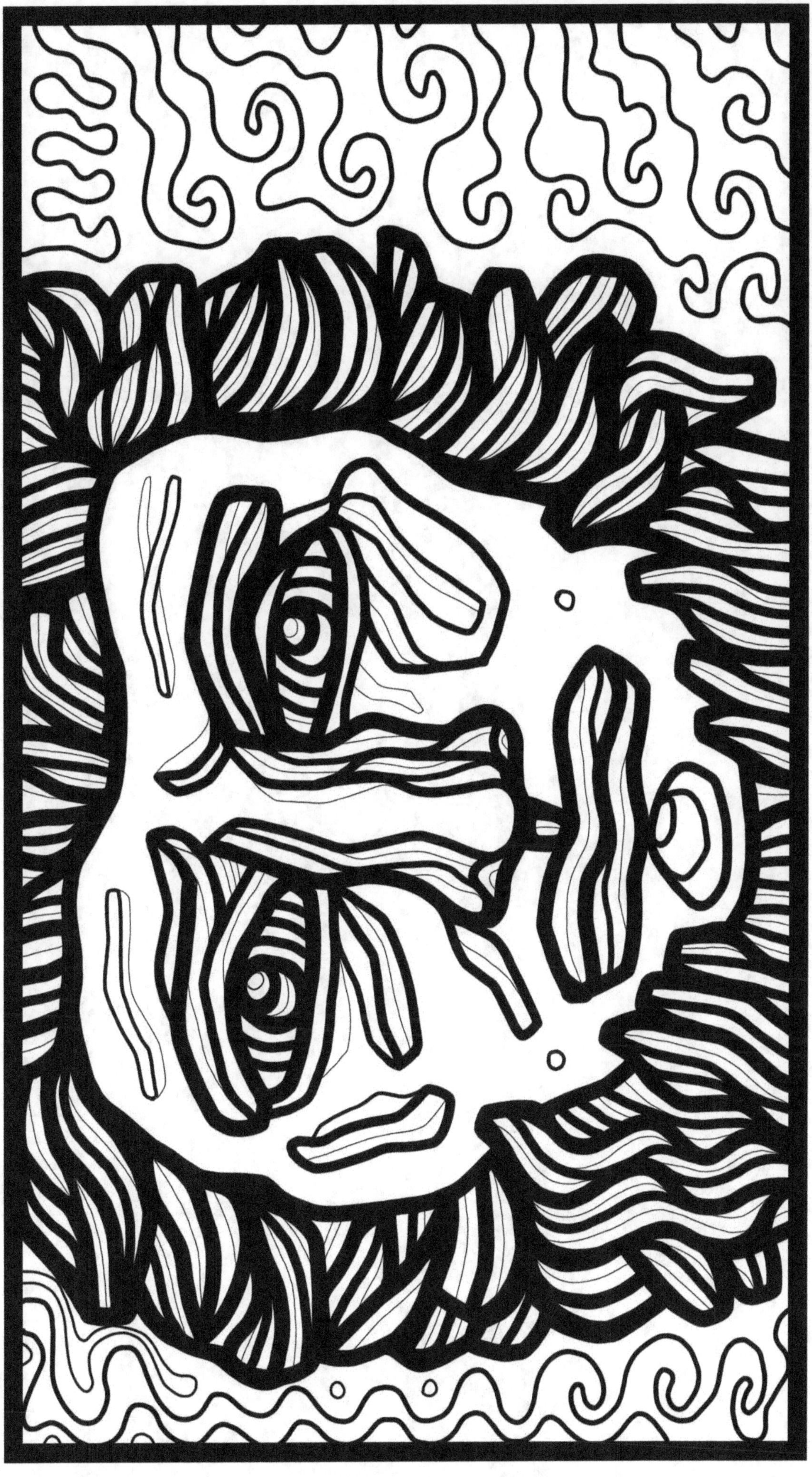

THE END, THANK YOU.

MORE BOOKS:
631ART.COM

www.ingramcontent.com/pod-product-compliance
Lightning Source LLC
Chambersburg PA
CBHW080133240526
45468CB00009BA/2423
* 9 7 8 1 7 9 5 5 9 7 5 5 5 *